21st Century Essays On Homelessness

KIRSTEN ANDERBERG

DEDICATION

This book is dedicated to all of the children who have experienced the underbelly of American society through homelessness in their youth.

21st Century Essays on Homelessness

CONTENTS

PREFACE

The articles in this book were written by Kirsten Anderberg between the years 2004 – 2007. They have been published in various venues in the past, but this is the first publication of all of the articles in one anthology.

This book is published with the hopes that real estate greed will someday cease and that the fiction of land ownership will someday quit creating homelessness, poverty, hunger and war.

1 THE PRIVILEGE OF PRIVACY AND HOMELESSNESS

Written February 5, 2007

When I've been homeless, the hardest part has been the lack of privacy. The privilege of privacy is something many take for granted, but for those of us who have experienced homelessness firsthand, privacy becomes a mindset, rather than a physical reality. And that fortress of privacy within one's mind adds to the wide chasm between the housed and the homeless, often making homeless people seem "crazy" to housed folks. And when one has been forced to make mental doors that shut, since physical doors to shut for safety are nonexistent, it is as if there is a change to one's soul.

Homeless people are burdened with an obligation to hide, while given no privacy. Often homeless folks learn to "hide" mentally, like an ostrich hiding its head in the sand. It is a sanity tactic, even if it appears "nuts" to people with privacy privilege. The ability to shut a door with 4 walls is something many take for granted. Such privacy affords a human a moment to let down his guard, emotionally and physically. Physical privacy allows a person some rest, a moment to rejuvenate. But homeless folks never get that moment to relax, let down their guard, and rejuvenate. Kept on alert at all times, guarding all belongings, and self, in public, is exhausting, both physically and mentally.

To many people who have been homeless and lived on the street, getting away from people is their greatest dream. Already tainted as untouchables or the unwanted, people have collectively left a bad taste in many homeless people's hearts. And the constant exposure to other people is as eroding as any physical weather elements. Honestly, I found the constant exposure to people to be much more dangerous to my mental and physical health than the exposure to cold, rain, etc., when I was homeless.

This human need for privacy to regroup, to heal and recover from life's traumas, to feel safe, emotionally and physically, is something the "housing first" movement understands. A movement to house the homeless, with no strings attached, is a big step forward, being promoted by organizations such as Pathways to Housing aka PTH (http://www.pathwaystohousing.org).

PTH says it is inhumane to hold homeless people hostage with obligations to get stable before receiving help with housing. And it is true that many people with housing, and large incomes as well, cannot conquer their drug addiction and mental health issues. So to ask low-income folks who are homeless to conquer those demons first, as a prerequisite for housing, truly is cruel and inhumane.

PTH believes "only housing cures homelessness." That sounds so simple, but it is quite profound. They are saying that the issues of drug abuse, mental illness and homelessness are separate. They are saying those 3 issues entail separate remedies, and that the remedy for homelessness is actually quite simple compared with the other issues. Curing homelessness merely entails providing stable and secure housing for the homeless. PTH provides permanent housing of the tenant's choice, and then offers voluntary, not mandatory, programs to help tenants with other issues, such as drug addiction or depression.

PTH understands that when homeless, survival is first and foremost. Self-improvement takes a back seat to survival, when homeless. By giving homeless people some privacy, some alone time, and some safety, and by giving them a physical door, so they can open the mental doors they shut long ago, "housing first" programs are healing the souls of homeless folks.

I am saying I believe the thing homeless people often crave, miss, and desire most, is PRIVACY. Often privacy is the most necessary missing element for the recovery of a homeless person's hope and faith, and a return of their dignity. Often privacy is the missing prerequisite for peace in the souls of many homeless people. The privacy becomes a symbol of safety, even. We come to know we are safe, because we have privacy.

Although many homeless people appear to be anti-social, due to shutting emotional/mental doors to compensate for no physical doors to shut, I think there is a process to opening back up to people, to trusting again, to re-integration...and ironically, getting alone time, and privacy, can be the first step to overcoming anti-social behaviors.

I was a homeless kid: in institutions, foster care, as a homeless teen. The message I got was I was an unwanted party crasher on this planet. I was taught to hide myself in this society as a child. I have been homeless as an adult in my past, as well. I have reoccurring nightmares involving doors. I will rent an apartment, move in, then realize the front door has a 10 inch gap under it, between the floor and its bottom, making it easy to enter under the door, even when locked. Or I move into an apt. and the front door literally falls off when I shut it, as if it has no hinges, etc. My father broke down my locked bedroom door in a drunken rage in my teens. As a child in MacLaren Hall, a torturous holding place for unwanted and severely abused children in Los Angeles, I had no privacy, no doors to lock out the violent guards and children who were acting out what they had seen adults do to them. Doors are a big thing to me....and many others like me.

Locking doors are a privilege. If you don't have physical locking doors, you will make mental locking doors, as exemplified by the "bag lady," who appears oblivious to those around her in public. Mental doors are a form of sanity, not insanity. And as I've said, and as people at Housing First programs have come to understand, homeless people cannot safely open locked mental doors until there are safe physical doors to replace them.

"What is a room without a door, which sometimes locks or stands ajar? What is a room without a wall, to keep out sight and sound from all? And dwellers in each room should have the right to choose their own design, and color schemes to suit their own, though differing from mine." - Pete Seeger

2 MENTAL HOSPITALS AS HOMELESS SHELTERS

Written in 2005

Many homeless people use mental hospitals to survive the winter. This has been an accepted fact for as long as mental institutions, insane asylums, and psychiatric hospitals have been in existence. In the earlier "insane asylum" days, homeless people were committed to these "sanatoriums" against their will, merely for being homeless. But I guess we saw thresholds come into play and as homeless populations soared, the mandatory mental hospital stays for the homeless populations also dropped, as the state could not keep up with the demand. To reduce mental hospital services to the homeless populations, many states began to frame the help as unnecessary "welfare," as did Ronald Reagan so superbly, instead of public health and/or protection, which people willingly paid for. Archaic insane asylums, as well as modern state mental hospitals, always have a population of predominantly poor people, as families with wealth can usually afford to pay an attendant to stay with the "unruly" family member, often to avoid their namesake being "tainted" by public knowledge of their family member's situation. Most will agree that issues applicable to state mental hospitals always revolve around issues of the poor. So it is ironic, and not ironic, simultaneously, that nowadays, homeless people are trying to get into these institutions as shelter from the cold and for regular meals.

In SE Ohio, the "Athens Lunatic Asylum" opened in 1874, ready to accommodate 544 patients. By the 1950's, it had expanded to house approximately 2000 patients. According to the Athens Asylum's website (http://www.ohiou.edu/~ridges/About.html), "The reason for the ever increasing population was the lack of criteria for admittance; patients in the asylum included those that were epileptic, menopausal, alcohol and tubercular victims, and, also, seasonal visitors that otherwise would be homeless." Later, this same site says, "It was common for homeless people, tramps and hobos to become 'patients' of the asylums seasonally for shelter and food, and then "elope," or slip away when the good weather returned. Families would often submit their elderly relatives to asylums because they lacked the resources or time to deal with them appropriately. The problem with overcrowding developed because the institutions had no established criteria for accepting or rejecting patients into their care. Rapid growth in populations caused patient care to suffer. In the Athens Asylum the patient population jumped from 200 to nearly 1800, with an insignificant alteration in staffing. The community found that these institutions were an easy means to remove unwanted people from society. There was no effort to provide any other programs or support, because the state was paying for the asylum."

Marie Balter is a famous ex-mental hospital resident turned activist, who seems to have used the nearby mental hospital in Danvers, Mass., as a child, as an escape from the abusive household she grew up in. This makes me think that not only are homeless folks using mental hospitals as a safety net, but abused children are using them as an escape from homelessness and abusive homes, as well (while ironically being committed against their will to these institutions for "acting out" against said abuses, in other circumstances). I came from an abusive home and was homeless at age 16, so I looked back to see if I had approached mental hospitals for help when I was on the street as a youth. I realized, to my own surprise, honestly, that I had. I went to a mental hospital in California and asked them to take me as a patient, at age 16 in 1977. They asked if I was going to kill myself. I said no, that I was just homeless, with no family, and really depressed, and not sure how to pick up the pieces…and they told me I could make an appointment with a doctor for a later date, but I would not be admitted to the mental hospital. I remember leaving confused, thinking I could not even get admitted to a mental hospital! Somehow that seemed like a low low!

I was on the bus on Nov. 2, 2004, on a rainy Seattle day, when I overheard two people talking in the back of the bus. A man who identified himself as homeless was talking to a woman. He said he was fighting to get admitted to a local mental hospital, Fairfax. He said he had gotten in trouble with the law several times and also fought with the Veterans Administration over slights in his check for not doing what they told him to do. He said it was getting cold sleeping on the streets as winter approached and he hoped to get into the mental institution soon.

The woman asked what he got at the mental hospital that made him want to go there. He said, "They feed me real well." She said, "Would you live there just for the food?" He said, "They feed us well, I have a warm and dry bed, I am given counseling, and I am given 20 mg. of Valium every four hours if I want it." He said, "I am ½ crazy, no, maybe ¾ crazy, so it is okay." Next the woman said she was on her way to vote. The man asked who she was voting for. She said "Bush." He said, "Good girl."

I have always been terrified of mental institutions ever since I went on a field trip with a psychology class in high school to Camarillo State Mental Hospital, outside of Los Angeles. But I see, in retrospect, that I also was desperate enough in my teens when kicked onto the streets, to go to them for help. People do not go to mental hospitals for housing as a first choice. It is a last ditch option, when people are down and out, cold and hungry. It seems a shame to me that in a society as rich as America, we still have abused children, the poor and the homeless using mental hospitals for a warm, dry bed and a meal. It is a reflection on the failures of capitalism and "civilization," in my opinion.

3 AMERICAN "INSANE ASYLUM" HISTORY: GIVING NAMES TO NUMBERED GRAVES

Written in 2004

In 1997, an ex-mental hospital patient and activist, Pat Deegan, was walking her dog on the property of the then closed Danvers State Mental Hospital, located 30 minutes north of Boston. Danvers State Hospital opened in 1878, and has been closed since the early 1990's. She came upon an overgrown, abandoned cemetery, with only numbers on small round markers. Soon she found a second overgrown cemetery of numbered markers. (It was estimated there was about 40 years of overgrowth covering the cemeteries). Pat soon began facilitating slide shows of what she had seen, as well as organizing ex-patients for field trips and action.

The Danvers State Memorial Committee (DSMC) was soon formed thereafter, with the goal of restoring and properly memorializing the two Danvers State Hospital cemeteries. The DSMC nominated a steering committee of 12 people, of whom most were ex-patients. Marie Balter, a famous mental hospital patient turned activist, whose story was told in a movie with Marlo Thomas playing Marie, called "Nobody's Child," was one of those on the steering committee. One of the first hurdles they faced was determining who was responsible for cleaning up, and then long term maintenance of, the cemeteries. A decision was made to press the state to be accountable for the cemeteries. But there were still problems, such as the Dept. of Mental Health (DMH) had the records for the closed hospital, and a private entity was soon to buy the state hospital property, and then the activists would have to get permission to clear the cemeteries from them, etc. The DSMC also reports there was considerable anger present at early meetings. Many were still very angry at past abuses they had suffered at Danvers State. They were adamant that the truth, not the sanitized version, of the hospital's past be told. Some members of the DSMC felt the group was not the place for that anger. But the group did not shun those who were angry, and instead were able to harness their anger into a powerful force. Due to these discussions, the DSMC decided to ask for a formal apology as part of the return of dignity to those buried with only numbers on the hospital grounds.

The DSMC has left a well-detailed map (http://dsmc.info/work.shtml), so to speak, of how a grassroots organization got bureaucracy to deal with the issue of these unmarked graves, as well as concise instructions on how to memorialize unmarked graves in your own area on a local level. The DSMC was formed in 1997, and their website addresses issues such as how they organized themselves, and how they found "room for anger," as well as how they worked through conflict. They detail how they sought out media coverage to break gridlock with bureaucracy, and used field trips to boost the group's morale. The group also became a lightning rod for activism that ex-patients had not had access to before. People who had writings about their experiences at Danvers, who had made art about their stay at Danvers, for example, began to emerge. They became active in legislative lobbying, as well as testifying before legislature, building coalitions, developing public education and outreach, etc. By 1999, the issue had gone from a local to state status. State legislators began introducing bills to have all cemeteries at state facilities restored and properly memorialized, which would affect other cemeteries on state facility lands, such as prisons, state hospitals, public health hospitals and state "schools for the retarded." When the DSMC organized testimony for one legislative session, all the supporters wore a button with the picture of grave marker #115. A lone cement round marker, with a number, on many people's lapels, was a powerful symbol. As a DSMC member testified, she said "Who is #115? We don't know." Other supporters present held up effective pictures that were enlarged, of the cemeteries in decay.

It is not clear why these headstones contained a number only. Some believe the numbers were used to protect families from the stigma of having a "mentally ill" person in their family. Another argument raised addresses patient confidentiality. Some people feel it is a breach of confidentiality to share either a list of former patents buried at the hospitals, or to put their names on the grave markers. The first question raised is whether the reason for the confidentiality is shame and stigma associated with mental illness, and if that is the reason, then the names could help fight that stigma. A second argument for names replacing numbers is that state "schools for the retarded" in the same states that used numbers for mental patients, often put whole names on their former patients' gravestones. If there was no breach of confidentiality in naming patients at state "schools for the retarded" on their gravestones, why would such a breach occur when applied to the state's mental hospital patients? Regarding a breach to release a list of names of former patients, the benefit outweighs the risk, is one argument. The DSMC, for instance, is a well-organized group of ex-patient activists with a coherent plan, timeline, funding, etc. They say they want to offer dignity to other ex-patients who were not respected or treated with the societal norm at burial. Some say the numbers on the graves were just the quickest, cheapest way to mark the headstones. I suspect indifference was the cause. Indifference on the part of the hospital staff, and indifference on the part of society, and indifference on the part of their own families who put them there in the beginning and left them there in the end. Indifference and stigma. Hospital carpenters made coffins for patients who passed on in the beginning, but eventually the state bought the coffins and numbered markers at Danvers.

Besides leaving an invaluable record for others regarding grassroots organizing and direct action campaigns, the DSMC also leaves us a clear written document about how they got the graves properly marked with names and dates, how they changed laws, etc. In 1999, the DSMC began looking at a strategy for naming the buried. The issue of confidentiality was raised and the committee decided that putting names on grave stones was not an issue of confidentiality, but rather one of respect. Patients had not been asked if they wanted to have their name on their grave. It was hospital policy to put numbers on graves and that policy most probably came out of a sense of shame and a desire to protect families from the "shame of mental illness," the committee argued. For example, an old letter was found during research into Dixmont Mental Hospital, written by the family of a patient, upon being informed that their relative died at Dixmont. The letter told the hospital never to write them again and that they would not be coming for the body.

The DSMC has been working with many entities for years now to fund and facilitate the clearing of brush and landscaping of the cemeteries, as well as paying for long-term maintenance, proper headstones, and proper research into the names where records were lost. With 768 graves to identify, the task before the DSMC was daunting. They found an old cemetery ledger with 150 names corresponding to grave numbers. For others, they discovered the death certificate records for the town of Danvers listed Danvers State Hospital as the place of death of many patients, and often it said they were buried at the "asylum cemetery" or "the state hospital cemetery," but the grave numbers were not recorded. Finally, in 2000, the brush was cleared from the Danvers State cemeteries, and at a celebration, a bulb was planted next to each numbered grave, to blossom in the spring. So far they have identified 542 of the 677 people buried in the larger of the two cemeteries. A memorial wall of some sort is planned for those whose names are never found.

In addition to Danvers State, another 10,000 numbered graves are located on former state hospital, school, and prison grounds across Massachusetts. At Bridgewater State Hospital's former complex, a cemetery behind the chapel and morgue has 50 markers and although there is no list of the names of those buried there, it has been asserted they were former DMH patients. Foxboro State Hospital has two cemeteries, which buried approximately 1,100 former DMH patients in its cemeteries, but they are not on the hospital grounds. They are about 1/8 mile from the hospital. The names and corresponding grave numbers are lost, but the stones do have their DMH number on the back of each numbered marker, so that may help eventually. Gardner State Hospital is a former DMH facility with as many as 600 unidentified former DMH patients buried in their cemetery. Grafton is another closed DMH hospital, with its cemetery off site also. 1,041 former DMH clients are buried there. Their 3 acre cemetery has a complete list of the names and corresponding grave numbers. Taunton State Hospital sent its DMH patients that died to the pauper graves at 2 local cemeteries, thus no one knows how many were buried there. The Westboro State Hospital is still open, and no cemeteries have been found on site. The whereabouts of their former patients who died are still being researched, including plots listed as "State Hospital Plots" at a nearby local cemetery. As you can see, this issue is not limited to Danvers, and it is not limited to Massachusetts either.

Another mental asylum with numbered, instead of named, graves on site, is the site of the old "Athens Lunatic Asylum" in SE Ohio. When it opened, in 1874, the Athens Lunatic Asylum was built to house 544 patients on 150 acres. But by the 1930's, the asylum had expanded to 1000 acres and was housing 1600 patients. The asylum had about 2000 patients in the 1950's, when it held its highest patient population. According to the Athens Asylum's website (http://www.ohiou.edu/~ridges/About.html), the hospital took in a large number of seasonal patients who were homeless during winter months, and they would leave when warmer weather returned.

The hospital grounds at Athens hosted gardens and a dairy, as well as orchards, a farm, and vineyards, and became nearly self-sufficient. Fresh water on the property came from springs and wells but as the patient population increased wells had to be dug. They also had to buy heating coal and kerosene for lanterns used in all the buildings until 1895. I would assume kerosene lamp-lit asylum tunnels could be pretty scary at night. The weird shadows the windows paint on the afternoon walls gives one the creeps, even when abandoned now for years. The way the hospital was built, you could only exit and enter from the center building.

Like Danvers, the cemeteries on site contain those patients who died at the asylum. It is unclear whether there are two or three cemeteries at Athens. The graves are in military-style rows. Although the graves only have numbers, there are burial records with the patient names matched to the grave numbers, dating back to 1880, although the asylum opened in 1868. The death records are divided into males and females. So there is a male number "7," and a female number "7" grave. The only way to tell which #7 is a woman and which is a male is to look at where the original gravestone was placed. In the beginning, it is believed the burial grounds were segregated by sex, although in time, it is believed both sexes became intermingled in the burial grounds. Another anomaly is that the first female death, #1, is recorded as being buried in 1880, yet the first male burial records begin with patient #64 in 1880. There is no record of who the first 63 men buried there are. In the death records were the patient names, number on grave, along with a date, and there was room for comments such as the religion of the patient, whether they received a colored or private headstone, if and when the body had been taken from the site and who conducted funeral services. Oddly, some private headstones with names and information were placed behind the numbered graves on the grounds, and it is suspected these were placed there by family members or loved ones. There are also some red headstones from the state, with a number, a name, and dates of birth and death. The first of these state stones with names was numbered #716. There are also some records of male patients' bodies being "donated" to Ohio University and these male patients received no numbering. The last number for a female death entered was #847, and the last number for a male death entered was #1117, in 1972, when the hospital closed.

Minnesota is another area where unmarked graves are being replaced with proper names of deceased patients. In 2003, named grave markers were placed on 128 graves in the Oak Knoll Cemetery in Willmar, MN, while tens, if not hundreds more unmarked graves of former residents of the Willmar State Hospital were found on site. In 2003, in East Central MN, a celebration was held to honor and celebrate all 354 former Cambridge State Hospital Residents who now have their names on their graves. By 2000, it was discovered this was a problem of epidemic proportions in America. Tewksbury State Hospital in Mass. recently discovered an estimated 10,000 unmarked graves in its 3 cemeteries. The former Milledgeville State Hospital in Georgia is working on the restoration of 30,000 graves in its cemeteries. Dixmont was a mental institution in Western PA, named after Dorothea Dix, famous mental health rights activist. Dixmont opened in 1862 and closed in1984. More than 1,300 graves, marked and numbered on small stones, can be found in the woods on the Dixmont property. The state of Pennsylvania continues to preserve a 1-acre cemetery where 1,300 former patients are buried. Many states in the U.S. have begun to restore state hospital cemeteries with local grassroots organizations, often inspired by the DSMC, leading, at the helm. Activists in this area have pretty clear goals. In general, they are asking for: 1) Funding for clearing of overgrowth and landscaping of the cemeteries, 2) Grave markers with Names and Dates, not numbers as identification, 3) Funding for continued maintenance of cemeteries, 4) A Public Apology from state officials. Some additionally are asking for a memorial or museum space on the cemetery grounds to help society from repeating past mistakes, and to ensure ongoing support for the project.

In the 1800's, people were being put into mental institutions for all kinds of things: wives and daughters who did not obey their husbands or fathers were sent there, as were "angry people," alcoholics, people with depression, homeless people, women in menopause, and certainly disobeying the status quo was grounds for questioning one's mental health also. From 1840 to 1890, reports claim the amount of people hospitalized for mental illness leapt from 2,500 to 74,000. There were reportedly over 500,000 patients in mental institutions in America in 1960. Burying these large numbers of patients became laborious for the institutions. At Northampton State Hospital (NSH), which opened in 1858, most of its patients were buried on the grounds, up until approximately the 1920's. But patients at NSH had no family to claim them, and when died became state property, so in the 1920's, these unclaimed bodies became cadavers for medical schools via the state, eliminating some of their cemetery needs.

With severe overcrowding, more patients had to be restrained in the hospitals. And more shock treatment, as well as extreme treatments such as lobotomies, came into vogue around the 1930's. As lobotomies became more quick and easy, "traveling lobotomists" came through towns. One "lobotomist" of that era performed 3,000 lobotomies by himself. Shock therapies, such as insulin shock therapy, electroshock therapy, etc., only subsided once drug therapy was introduced on a large scale. As more people were drugged, and as society changed its views on mental illness, menopause, human rights, etc., less people were institutionalized for their epilepsy, menopause, alcoholism, tuberculosis and "seasonal homelessness." But as more of the drugged patients were sent away from the hospitals' nearly self-sufficient farms, gardens, etc., they were sent away from sustainable lifestyles, into city labor pools. Additionally, in 1972, the patient labor laws were enacted, prohibiting the use of patient labor for farming and other chores without pay on hospital grounds, which had good and bad sides to it. At one point, 3 out of 4 patients were released from Athens, going to family homes, nursing homes and half-way houses. Homeless numbers soared. By 1986, U.S. mental institutions had 100,000 less mental patients than it had before the push for drugs instead of institutionalization. And as you can see from statements made above, homeless people often ended up at mental hospitals for food and shelter in earlier years, so homelessness and mental hospitals are inexorably intertwined throughout history. At times when we are talking about an unmarked grave in back of a mental institution, we are really talking about a grave of a homeless person who had nowhere else to go during a cold winter, not a person with "mental illness."

The reason that these state hospital cemeteries are being restored is not just about history, it is about the present and future. It is about making sure that people who die in state institutions are not marginalized any further. It is a cry to end the anonymity of the state's institutional patients in life and death. Pursuing dignity and respect for those who went before us can be a way of respecting ourselves today. Not only is it empowering for current and ex-psychiatric patients to see the community coming together to honor these previously unnamed dead, but it gives us all a moment to reflect upon what these numbered grave markers represent and how society has interplayed with the "mentally ill" in our recent past. It gives us a moment to reflect upon the stigma that mental illness has held for so long.

Much of the cemetery reclamation has to do with individual healing, as well as community healing. Just as an overgrown, disheveled state hospital cemetery full of numbered markers makes one feel badly, to see a well-cared-for, community supported cemetery honoring the past lives of mental hospital patients is an inspiration. The cemeteries that have been reclaimed give people, especially ex-patients, a place to grieve, to remember, to return, as well as a place to collectively bring closure to painful episodes in lives. As one member of the Danvers State Memorial Committee, Mark Giles, has said about restoring state hospital cemeteries: "This is about respect. We have been neglected for too long...It has been said that no families have come forward to claim their relatives buried in these cemeteries. WE are their family."

Within the pages of the DSMC website you can learn more about the issues related to advocacy for state hospital cemetery restoration and how you can help identify and restore a cemetery in your area. They say the best way to get started doing state hospital cemetery restoration is to get out there with a camera, find the cemeteries, photograph them, and then bring that information to the local community and especially to ex-patients of the hospital. They stress the process as being as important as the end product. It may be easier for the hospital or state to restore the cemeteries quietly, but to involve ex-patients in the planning and restoration is a novel way to approach healing for several communities involved.

When looking for a cemetery at local state hospitals in your area, the experts recommend finding out the history of the hospital. State hospitals established before 1900 usually had cemeteries on grounds. They recommend talking to ex-patients, as they often know the grounds very well. Old employees and local elder clergy can also have old knowledge of the grounds. If you cannot find the cemetery on the grounds, ask local cemeteries if they had pauper graves for the state hospital decades prior. Sometimes local cemeteries had "pauper fields" in the back of the cemetery, with numbered markers, just like at the hospital cemeteries. And some hospitals cremated the patients, so there is no cemetery to be found. Activists recommend using slideshows of cemeteries found locally and of cemeteries abroad that have been forgotten and then restored, to gather community interest. Field trips to the site of the unkempt cemeteries also helped establish commitment to the projects. When involving ex-patients in this activism, often patients will get angry. That anger can be funneled into positive action for change. The activists recommend monthly meetings, as well as allowing for anger and different personal reasons for wanting to participate in such a project.

4 THE "NEW POOR" VERSUS THE "OLD POOR": WHO GETS PRIORITIZED?

Written in 2004

We have all heard the terms "old money," and "new money" with regards to familial wealth. "Old money" is perceived to be more noble, and more dignified in stature somehow. "New money" is considered superficial, transitory, or even happenstance. These same concepts can be applied to the poor. And what is interesting is the way society will try to separate out the "new poor" from the "old poor" when determining who to give aid to. The "new poor" are treated as more deserving of help. And indeed, the "new poor" are easier to help, as they are not entrenched in poverty from all angles yet. The "old poor" often have harder attitudes and edges due to the prolonged crisis of poverty, and often are less graceful with the hands that feed them. Their "polish" in dealing with charity and welfare agencies wore off over the years, as they identified their fate as a side effect of a malfunctioning capitalist society, not a fate borne of their innate inferiority or laziness. So "new poor" happens to someone and it is not their fault, so we give them lots of help with no stigma. But the "old poor" create their own poverty, thus they should not be helped. That constructively, is the philosophy involved. We see time and again, that Americans love to help those who are not the most in need of help. I do not know why that is. But it seems to be the American way.

We see that society is eager to help home owners who lose estates in Florida from tropical storms, or from fires in Malibu Canyon in California. But society is not so eager to help those who never owned a home to begin with. I remember reading in the New York Times, just after 9/11/01, about a new widow who had people give her money so she could keep her pool cleaner coming, as if this was some heroic gesture on the part of her friends and strangers. Yet no one seems to care about the widow living on the streets of NYC, who cannot afford food or shelter, much less a pool or pool cleaner. Oprah recently gave away new cars to every studio audience member, to mostly middle class folks. If she had given a new car to an entire audience of homeless people, she would have given them transportation, a place to sleep/home, and a place to keep food, clothing and belongings.

The rush to help everyone but the truly poor is an interesting phenomenon. Perhaps people are doing an unspoken triage. People are thinking there are poor folks who will survive without our help. Then there is a group that will not survive without our help, such as the 9/11 widow who would have had a dirty pool lest she clean it herself which is preposterous.

And then there are the poor folks who have sunk too far into poverty to save sans huge, sustained, long-term efforts. In the last class, we have truly poor people that we abandon altogether, such as people who have been homeless for 10 years. The middle group only requires token aid, and thus is the maximized venture for those wanting immediate glory or brownie points for helping the poor. It requires the least input for the maximum accolades. And appears to be America's choice group for charity.

In the aftermath of Florida's recent barrage of tropical storms, I am sure the "old poor" are slipping under the radar of powers that be, to utilize programs set up for the "new poor," aka programs no one would facilitate for the "old poor." I saw this in full play after the 7.1 earthquake in 1989 in Santa Cruz, CA, that collapsed the Oakland freeway. Santa Cruz at that time had a large homeless population. Then the quake hit. And suddenly middle class families were temporarily homeless, due to structural damage to the homes they owned. A shelter was set up at the Santa Cruz Civic Auditorium, with beds, blankets, food and water. We had torrential rains after the quake, so the homeless population showed up to use these cots, dry blankets, food, etc., these things that were set up for middle class quake victims apparently. There was a public uproar when suburban families complained about having to sleep next to "bums" in the shelter. A move was made to separate out the "old poor" from the "new poor," but it failed. The "old poor" just lied, saying they had been living somewhere that was now ruined. I remember the end result being something like the homeless population took over most of that shelter and the middle class people went somewhere else, probably motels, and the shelter was shut down earlier than it would have been if it had been used by middle class families instead of homeless folks.

This also played out in the Northridge earthquake in 1994. (Yes, I have a propensity for earthquake epicenters). My building collapsed and my son and I needed clothing, food, shelter, etc. immediately. The Red Cross required I prove my home address and that my building had collapsed. How I was supposed to hunt that down, without being allowed into my home, the day after the quake, was beyond me. Finally, a fire chief came into the Red Cross station I was at, and announced every building on my block was condemned, so anyone living in that area was automatically cleared for services. I was finally able to prove my address from something I was able to get out of my car. But if I had been homeless and hungry, without papers to prove I had not just been homeless before the quake, the Red Cross apparently would not have been interested in helping us at all.

As conditions degraded in the San Fernando Valley in the days after the Northridge quake, water and food were a hassle to obtain. Lines of people wound around blocks waiting to buy food and water from grocery stores. Since the stores were damaged themselves and aftershocks kept on coming, customers were not allowed to go inside the stores. You would finally get to the front of the line, give a list to a store clerk, they would go risk their lives in a building too unstable to allow the public in, and would bring what you wanted up front and you paid in cash. Another option was to wait in long lines at local high schools for the National Guard to give you 5 gallons of water to put in a container you brought to the site. I was not enthused about standing in the hot sun for hours to get water. I wondered if I drove my old Dodge Dart to a part of town with more money, if I would find water easier. And sure enough, I did.

Unlike the long lines for food and water in the San Fernando Valley, the National Guard was literally sitting at I-5 off ramps giving out free cases of bottled water to families in the middle class white suburbs of Santa Clarita, which is only a few miles north of the San Fernando Valley. Santa Clarita had suffered hard blows from the quake too, it was not like they were in an area with little to no damage. They had enough damage to bring in the National Guard with water and to warrant Red Cross stations be set up there. But somehow their water was flowing freely, while people were fighting for water down in San Fernando, which has a large Latino population and a larger low-income population. In addition to the cases of water just sitting by the off ramps in Santa Clarita, the Red Cross stations there also had an abundance of water and encouraged me to take a case of bottled Evian water with me when I left. Unlike the Red Cross shelters in San Fernando which were full, the Santa Clarita shelters were completely empty. Why the Red Cross could not transport the extra water and beds from Santa Clarita to San Fernando is beyond me. Additionally, why the National Guard was literally sitting by road sides with cases of water when they could have driven those cases of water into San Fernando is beyond me as well. But this seems to be the pattern. Money and aid is given to that middle group in social triage first and foremost.

We saw this type of thing during the Depression Era in America as well. As more and more people became unemployed, homeless and hungry, the lines between the "new poor" and the "old poor" blurred. Many efforts were made to separate the two for aid. And just as we see today, somehow business ends up as one of those in line for aid as well, as masses grow poorer. Just like Bush's tax break for the rich in America nowadays, we saw Hoover's response to the Depression was to create the Reconstruction Finance Corporation, which gave federal aid to "agriculture, commerce and industry." Apparently, big business becomes the "new poor" worthy of aid at some point as well!

When a tropical storm creates homelessness, there is help available. When an earthquake creates homelessness, there is help available. But when capitalism creates homelessness, who do you call to cover that emergency? And when would that aid be able to cease? After the 1994 quake, I was stunned to find one of the pieces of furniture that the Federal Emergency Management Agency (FEMA) felt was an essential, that had to be replaced, even at government expense, was a television! When folks fill out their loss forms for FEMA now after these Florida storms, they will be asked if they had a TV. If they say yes, and they qualify for FEMA aid, FEMA will buy them a new TV. Priorities such as these are both telling and predictable. When given the choice, it appears most Americans would prefer to help the "new poor" over the "old poor." People really need to think about this concept of the "new poor" and the "old poor" to assess their own motives for helping the poor.

Why were we willing to give endless money to upper-middle class commodities brokers' families who suffered after the 9/11 tragedy, but not to wives of sugar cane workers in Florida whose husbands suffer machete injuries at phenomenal rates without any health insurance, to feed America's sugar addictions? How do we choose who to help? How do we prioritize the needs of all poor people? Prioritizing new and old poverty expands beyond the microcosm of America. It extends out to who we help internationally, in the macrocosm, as well. Which countries are prioritized for aid from America and why? Certainly those in the most dire need do not shoot to the top of the list for help. We need to take some time out to seriously study our priorities and motivations regarding aid to the poor, in the microcosm of America, and in the macrocosm of the world, with relation to these artificial divisions between the classes of the "new poor" and the "old poor."

5 ONCE YOU'VE BEEN HOMELESS, YOU CAN NEVER GO BACK

Written in August 2006

I was riding the bus today, lost in thought, when the bus pulled up to a stop and I looked out the window I was leaning against to see several women, with their baggage and small children, sitting on the pavement in a parking lot, looking weary and forlorn. I was immediately overcome with a familiarity; it reminded me horribly of my mom and me, when I was a child. I immediately realized this was a pick up spot for homeless shelters. As my bus rolled on, I saw the next block was lined with women, young and old, carrying their bags, hovering around, looking agitated, anxious, hot, worn out, and desperate, waiting outside the YWCA in downtown Seattle, to see if they will have shelter tonight (as local shelters cannot accommodate all of the women who need shelter nightly). By the time we had rolled past that block, I was in tears. I looked around me on the bus. It seemed no one even noticed what was outside our windows for the full length of the previous block.

"Once you have been homeless, you can never go back," I scribbled on a piece of scrap paper in my backpack. It occurred to me that perhaps many of the people on the bus around me did not understand what was going on out there on the street around the YWCA. It occurred to me that many, if not most, of those on the bus around me, had never been homeless and thus would not recognize that snippet of street reality that just was in our windows, for the painful scene of suffering it was. The way that scene got my attention was something outside the window triggered a very strong feeling in me, a bad feeling, a feeling of discomfort and anxiety, yet a familiar feeling, and I looked out. What I saw was me as a child, and my mom, fretting in worry, as we waited to figure out where we would sleep that night. I remember that feeling so much that I am still shaken hours later after feeling it again.

Outside the YWCA this evening, there were many women pacing around outside. And in the brief moments I looked at them through my bus window, I could remember the feeling of homelessness so vividly. And it is not a feeling I remember with any romance or sentimentality. I look at the periods I was homeless as pure survival and am glad I survived them. I do not look at them as adventurous times, at all. They are not fun memories, but scary, sad memories. Tonight I saw those mothers sitting out there, waiting, with those looks of surrender, those looks my mom had, like she had just given up...but I saw that look on the younger women out front of the YWCA too. Homelessness is incredibly hard work. It is a slippery slope. If you do not get out of homelessness quick enough, it becomes like quicksand, on several levels. Not only does it get hard to find somewhere to live and work without housing and clean clothing, etc., but there is this thing where you lose the will to try after a while and once that threshold is reached, all can just implode irreversibly. I feel my mom went over that threshold, and I have hovered at it, but thank god, never gone over it. I always got out of homelessness just before I gave up, is how I look at it. And when I see homeless women, frustrated, hot, weighed down with their bags, I think, "there but by the grace of god, go I."

People's reactions to poverty and homelessness can often be linked to the way they were raised. My dad was raised in a large single parent family in poverty during the Depression. My mom, in contrast, was raised in relative class privilege until her mid-30's when she went on welfare after the divorce. My dad was always embarrassed of his poverty and hated his mother for allowing them to be poor, basically. So his way of dealing with that, was to go into the Navy, get on the G.I.Bill, and to become an engineer. He then worked on making money and made sure to look away whenever poverty was anywhere near. He taught me not to look at poverty and to even shun it as well. But then my mom and I became poor, due to him not paying his child support and alimony and my mom being a single mom. My mom had taught me to be friends with poor kids, and also taught me that there was nothing wrong or "lesser" in poverty, as she had never been poor, and it really had nothing to do with her directly. Unlike my dad, who made every effort to look away from the poor and homeless people, my mom looked and spoke about the class oppression for what it was and condemned the powers that created poverty, such as racism, sexism, etc. before she was poor. I think that probably helped save her some sanity later when she became the poor.

My first homeless experience was with my mom when I was about 7. After that, I went through a series of institutional and foster care situations, then I went back to my mom. We were then thrown out of two different residences when we first moved to Seattle, when I was about 9 years old. It was scary being thrown out. I remember one time, we came home, and our bags and belongings were on the lawn and we were told to leave. We had no car or money. And my mom freaked out, broke down, it scared the hell out of me. And when I saw those women tonight in that parking lot, I felt that feeling my mom used to sweat out her pores. I could smell it through the bus' thick windowpane. That sorrow is a smell I can smell from far away.

There are many religious axioms that have stories of people who were ignorant of suffering on earth, but then they see it, smell it, touch it, and they cannot go back. They are not the same. And once this is seen, one's duties on earth and to each other change. If one did not help others when one did not know there was suffering, that is one thing. If one refuses to help others, when he does know about the suffering, and he could help alleviate it, then that is considered sinful. And due to my knowledge that women are on their last legs, lining up at shelters, in my town, every night, I am horribly uncomfortable. The others on the bus tonight had no feelings about it at all, it seemed. But me, it still is haunting me. I have just barely achieved sustainable housing in the last two years myself, and I would lose my housing if I brought a river of homeless folks into my apt, yet, the survivor guilt is very haunting and frankly, I am not sure what to do with it either.

It is true that once you have been homeless, you can never go back. I saw those women today in the parking lot as homeless mothers, when maybe the others on the bus just thought a bunch of women were hanging around together in a parking lot. But it was the grief on their faces that I recognized. And if you do not recognize that grief, having never been near it, then you have a sort of innocence, almost an excusable ignorance.

Not a day passes, that I do not thank the gods for my housing. I am serious. I have been homeless so many times this lifetime, that I do not take housing for granted, at all. As a matter of fact, that is why you can never go back. I never had fears of homelessness until I had been homeless. Until it happens to you, you do not really understand what being homeless entails and you do not think it has to do with you. When you realize it can happen to you, it looks very different than just some street scene you can roll by. I still have a haunting feeling about those women I saw tonight, and I can still feel my tears welling up as I even think about the front of the YWCA tonight. Because homelessness will forever be a wolf howling at my door, and I am always too close to being those women, which is why I cry, most probably. I cry for me, in them. And them, in me. I just think a world this full of riches, especially a country claiming to be the last remaining Superpower, can only be shamed for lines of homeless women on modern streets praying for a night's housing in desperation. And my survivor guilt is something I wrestle with every night, as I sleep in my bed, in my housing, that I know so many do not have.

6 HOMELESS KIDS AND THEIR PARENTS VS. THE WORLD

Written in 2006

I walked by a vacant lot of overgrown weeds today, in a suburban neighborhood of American single-family homes. The lot had a camper parked on it, with some things scattered around the front of the camper. A woman in her 40's came out of the camper, followed by a young boy about 12 years old. They were talking and interacting, but when I walked by, and the boy saw me, I saw shame all of a sudden come over his face.

I wanted to say, "Yeah, capitalism sucks! Power to the People! Eat the Rich!" or something to let that kid know that the shame was on the part of a rich, capitalist America that lets its poor go hungry and homeless, not on the poor. It is corporate greed that is responsible for homelessness. He did not need to convince me that his mom worked 24/7 just for them to survive. I know poverty is more than a full-time job. I wanted that kid to be proud, not ashamed, that he had survived in the face of poverty. I wanted him to see me respecting his mom. As Tupac Shakur said, if society rewarded high morals, his family would be rich. Many a good, hard-working family has struggled in poverty, while being called "freeloaders" and "lazy" by the very people who rip off the profits of their labor to keep them poor!

I cannot forget the haunting look the boy had in his eyes today. A look of internalized oppression, of shame, a desire to hide, and be invisible, for that moment. Even when someone who is not judging him negatively, but is instead loving him, walks by. I understand his emotional armor. Due to the way society treats the poor and homeless, the children of homeless adults often adopt a me-and-you against the world attitude. Hiding their family's homelessness from authorities, sleeping on the run, in one "illegal" place after another, homeless kids learn early to abhor police, and how to protect their parents from police and social workers, which is a huge responsibility for a young child. Many schools do not allow homeless kids to enroll. Many welfare offices refuse services to the homeless. Many social service agencies take children from homeless parents.

Remember Elizabeth Smart? She was kidnapped from her expensive home, and they finally found her living on the streets in Utah with a crazed homeless man and woman after a nationwide search for her? I saw an interview with her once she was back on her rolling acres of ranch property with her horses, back in her privileged lifestyle, playing her harp again. And one thing she said really stood out. I believe it was journalist Jane Pauley, who asked her what she had learned from the ordeal of being kidnapped. And Elizabeth's answer was stunning.

She said she's learned it is really hard to be homeless. She said you are hungry and cold all the time. I found it interesting that out of all of the mean things this kid could have said right then about the man and woman who kidnapped her, generalizing that the homeless are dangerous, she had instead seen compassion through all that, and had seen a glimpse of poverty that hopefully she will never forget. She said she did not understand why the people were homeless, but she did know it was horribly hard, so they must not want to be homeless.

Elizabeth Smart came from a family with money. So when they found her homeless on the street, she was whisked back to a big warm estate, with a loving family, all the food she could want, and a nation happy for her rescue. But every day little girls just like Elizabeth Smart go to sleep hungry and cold, and there is no nationwide search on for them, and they will not be brought home to a big warm estate. Additionally, they are hiding, and protecting their parents. And when you look at them, often times, you see adult pain in their eyes. Being a kid of a homeless adult, in a society that stigmatizes homeless people, has special obligations and traumas, that can grow a soul up real fast.

7 ADVERSE POSSESSION: HOW AND WHY PEOPLE SQUAT

Written on April 29, 2004

Adverse Possession, is squatting, basically, and it occurs in many countries, including the UK, the Netherlands, Scotland, Australia, Canada, Spain, Ireland…as well as in the US (New York City, Seattle, Boston, San Francisco, DC, Philadelphia…). Adverse possession, or legal squatting, has been in place in Europe since the 1400's, and in America since the 1600's. Reasons for squatting vary from political motivations to economic necessities. Some reasons for squatting are bringing community and media attention to the homeless and affordable housing crisis, to save lower income housing from demolition, to create community and lifestyle alternatives, to monkeywrench capitalism, and to challenge land ownership systems.

What would it take for squatting to be more widespread and tolerated? In the past, when the people were starving because landlords took ownership of the land and people had nowhere to farm food, eventually, the state let people TAKE land that was sitting idle to grow food as their own, to quell social uprising from starvation. It seems agrarian needs have been a reason, in the past, for overriding land owners' interests. The need for land to grow food on, as well as place your shelter upon, are survival needs, and when those survival needs are threatened, people are entrapped into dependencies upon outside third parties for food and shelter.

ADVERSE POSSESSION

Adverse Possession is an interesting legal concept. The theory is that when land is "unused," it does not benefit society, so if you are going to let your land sit wastefully, when someone else could use it and "improve" it, then it benefits society to let someone else use it. Of course this is legal fiction, because there would be no homeless people if this were easily applicable and enforceable. But the usual elements for adverse possession are exclusivity in the possession of the land (one identifiable entity uses it thus the fence, etc.), the possession of the property must be open and hostile to the owner, there is a time period of continuous occupancy that must be met before the title can be transferred, some states require you pay taxes on the land while adversely possessing it, etc. In Washington State, the Revised Code of Washington (RCW) 7.28.070 defines adverse possession as "Every person in actual, open and notorious possession of lands or tenements under claim and color of title, made in good faith, and who shall for seven successive years continue in possession, and shall also during said time pay all taxes legally assessed on such lands or tenements, shall be held and adjudged to be the legal owner of said lands or tenements, to the extent and according to the purport of his or her paper title. All persons holding under such possession, by purchase, devise or descent, before said seven years shall have expired, and who shall continue such possession and continue to pay the taxes as aforesaid, so as to complete the possession and payment of taxes for the term aforesaid, shall be entitled to the benefit of this section."

"Using" and "improving" property are the legal theories adverse possession are built upon. And those words are quite subjective. The legal definitions for land "improvements" for adverse possession tend to be a fence and a garden. American Indians roamed areas without fences and individual gardens, and lived off the land, thereby "using" it, but not via fenced-in individualized portions, thus many argued they were not using their land, and thus it was fine, via adverse possession, for Europeans to take American Indian land, placing the original inhabitants in a position of dependency. History is full of cultures becoming dependent upon outside third parties once land ownership is changed. Most often when a free people's land is fenced off and redirected by another, their culture is set askew from it. Sometimes this is intentional, such as the banning of native tongues and celebrations, and the use of reservations, by the American government after its taking of American Indian lands. With the claiming/taking of parts of the earth as one human's possession, or land ownership, comes class privilege and poverty. They follow hand in hand.

LAND OWNERSHIP THEORY

"Private property lives by grace of the law," writes Stirner. It is true that land ownership could not exist if the military and government did not protect the land owners. Or inversely, squatting would be more widespread without military and police action stopping it. When political or legal conditions change, squatting rises dramatically. During the 1974 leftist coup in Portugal, for example, 35,000 houses were squatted! If police laughed when land "owners" tried to claim one piece of land as theirs, imagine it. That would change everything. As I have said, land ownership requires force, and reinforcements. And it is also true that government change has been able to reallocate lands to different peoples over history. But usually only after a revolution, where the people pried the land out of the hands of someone else after long deadly struggles, such as in South Africa or Latin America. The fight over land, whether it is between countries and border lines, or between the people versus the government as during the agrarian squatter uprisings, reduces to individual land owner versus squatter, ready to take the land, in the microcosm of Adverse Possession. Adverse Possession is the American legal system's attempt at making squatting a civil process versus a criminal activity. But it falls short of that due to law enforcement at the local level, most often. After all, the land and business owners pay taxes, that fund the government and police, so for all constructive purposes, the tax payers pay the police and government as a security force to protect their property. Yet squatting laws are still unusually lax in many places due to the background of adverse possession in America.

Some have made analogies of our current land situation with a deserted island. Let's say a bunch of people arrive on an island after a shipwreck. Then one guy finds the area with all the fruit trees, ropes it off and tells the others that part of the island is his and no one else can use it. It is assumed the other island dwellers would laugh and not follow his concept! The analogy goes on further to explore the idea of the guy bringing a piece of paper saying he owned that part of the island. Again, it is assumed the others would only laugh. But then what if he returned with an army to reinforce his ownership on paper? Now things turn for the worst. He then can entrap islanders to do his labor for his food, or they can starve, or they can be jailed by the army if they try to get the land or food without paying the master...you can see how that is very similar to our current society where you either serve the land owners, or you are homeless, or you are in jail for trying not to be homeless.

Almost 3/4 of the world's private land is owned by just 2.5% of the landowners. In England, 1% of the population owns 75% of the land. In the US, 3% of population owns 95% of the private land. 80% of Americans own no land, and the top 22% of US land owners own 97% of American land (http://squat.net/archiv/anders/anarchist_squatting.html). And as people are pushed off their native lands, they can lose their knowledge of the landscape and native horticulture necessary for survival. Once cut off from the land, they are put into an involuntary welfare state, or made into an easy labor pool for capitalism, to keep paying the rents landowners demand. Additionally, many of the natural resources may disappear when fences are put up on land. Many have no interest in animal rights to lands, unless it is an animal population they exploit for money. Animals quit using areas they cannot access. The elephant herds were dramatically disrupted by fences and borders in Africa, wherein groups of elephants that used to socialize freely got trapped in areas, and only recently have actions been taken to try to open their paths up so they are not disjointed, but run unblocked, throughout the landscape, so elephants can go where they need to with their chosen clans. The issue of land ownership does not just affect people. Animals are very much affected by what people do with land.

Often industry does not care about the environment. They are willing to mine, dam, deforest, use nonsustainable farming, and contaminate the actual land itself, as a right of ownership. It does, also seem that the right to abuse is included in what "ownership" means. When people felt men owned women, it meant women had no rights and could be raped and abused without incident to the man. When people felt children were possessions owned by parents, children were sold, and abuse was allowed by the child's owner/parent, no police used to step in regarding child abuse, the child was the parent's sole property. When slaves were considered property, their masters had the "right" to abuse them. Even in lesser situations, employees often feel abused by their employers who own the businesses, and tenants feel abused by their landlords who own the land and rental properties. It seems the right to abuse is inherent in ownership qualities. And the right to abuse goes well with the need to use force to obtain and keep land ownership. Often it is the desire to abuse natural resources that fuels land wars in the first place, such as America's obsession with domination in the Middle East for American oil company profiteering.

It is also interesting to note that the government-owned lands in America are predominantly set aside for profits for private industry. They don't use the profits from timber sales from public forests for low income housing for the poor, but they do hand our forests by the acres over to private logging companies, and our lands and waters to nuclear companies, and our mountains to mining companies, all for private corporation profit. This scenario fueled many Latin American revolutions where the natural resources were later nationalized for use of the people. The American government is even willing to displace people with homes on lands near these private industrial projects...so the government not only does not let the poor use their own government's land to live on, but they displace families in the name of business, near government lands, increasing homelessness and poverty. Likewise, most hunger-related deaths are incurred by lack of access to food-producing land. As Francis Moore Lappé of Food First writes, "Hunger exists in the face of plenty; therein lies the outrage."

Frank Bardacke succinctly puts the land ownership issue into perspective in a paper he authored for a People's Park protest in Berkeley. It says that a long time ago American Indians lived in the area now referred to as Berkeley. These people had no concept of land ownership, when the Catholic missionaries took the land from them. Then the Mexican government took the land from the Catholic Church. The Mexican government made up some papers they signed saying they owned the land. No American Indians signed it. Then the American army was stronger than the Mexican army, so they took the land, drew up some papers saying they owned it, and forced the Mexicans to sign it. Then the American government sold the land, with their concocted paper land deeds, to "settlers," while American Indians were still claiming rights to the land. The American army killed the American Indians who made those claims. Then some rich men, who ran the University of California, bought the land, destroyed any houses built on the land, and now that land generates revenue for the rich men as...a parking lot.

SQUATTING HISTORY

Squats often take the form of community centers, as squats are often the result of community action. Also, it is a good idea to offer the neighborhood around the squat some preemptive benefits, to quell their complaints about the squat, if they were to occur. Additionally, present-day squatting alliances, such as "Homes Not Jails" (www.homesnotjails.org) in the US, who identify and set up squats for people who are homeless, and the Advisory Service for Squatters/ASS (http://www.squat.freeserve.co.uk) in England, have helped encourage and coordinate recent squats. In Barcelona, Spain, 1996, squatters took over a farm, refusing electricity to protest dams and nukes, and began a self-sufficiency project with organic farming and community workshops. They made their own bread, and sold it to other squatted centers in the area. It is not uncommon to find squats incorporating soup kitchens, libraries, workshops, free stores, zines and publications, work collectives, etc. in their goals and immediate actions. I heard a story about some punks working in Mexico with squatters. The punks had bright hair and wild clothes, and worked as teachers in their school. At first the community was hesitant to trust them, but in time, they grew to be family, and now when the kids from that settlement see a picture of a punk rocker, they point, and say "maestro," or "teacher."

Vancouver, B.C. (http://www.geocities.com/emithsilas/vansquat.html) has a rich squatting history. In the 1890's, a group of Finnish people built 70 stilt homes in a tidal flood area, and about 50 residents still live on the land without legal claim to it (as of April 2004). In 1946, 600 WWII vets in poverty took over the Hotel Vancouver, turning it into a hostel for up to 1,200 vets until 1948. A private owner bought the hotel/hostel and tore it down. In 1970, 300 homeless youth took over the Jericho Beach Hostel, and were evicted in a police battle that spread to the town. Twenty five people and six police officers were injured. Also in the 1970's, squatters tore down a fence and occupied a vacant site earmarked for construction eventually, and put up a tent and shack city that lasted about a year. In 1990, The Frances Street squats included several empty houses on one street. The squatters immediately tore down the fences between the yards, and set up a community space offering a free store, potlucks and get togethers.

One house was used as a women-only space. A rented house on the block not originally in the squat received an eviction notice, but they refused to leave or pay, and joined the squat themselves. In time, the Vancouver Police demanded the squatters leave. The squatters put up 6 foot high barricades, secured in-door defenses, and set fires in the middle of the streets. Squatters wore masks and helmets, but were evicted violently by 80 riot cops, 30 SWAT members, a bomb squad, earth-moving tractors to demolish the buildings, and more, according to published accounts. The public put more pressure on the federal government to create affordable housing after this event, and it also triggered more squats as well. A group called Direct Action Against Homelessness manifested a "Monster Squat," on Halloween 1997, in Vancouver, in an abandoned convalescent home. The place had been abandoned for over a year, yet the water still worked and the electricity was still connected (which, oddly, happens more than you would think!). They washed everything from walls to refrigerators, and groups donated food and chores. The space was immediately converted into a soup kitchen, and a community center for art, politics, social gatherings, and a safe space for the homeless.

During a one-weekend squat, people were well-fed, slept in warmth, and enjoyed community, in a positive environment. Police kicked in the doors finally, and forced the eviction.

The Page Street Squat in California is an interesting case where squatters, with the help of Homes Not Jails (http://www.sftu.org/hnj.html), took possession of the building, and began living in it in Feb 1993. The people who moved in were all very low-income and moved from homeless shelters into the building and shared meals. Since Homes Not Jails had occupied the home continuously for the statute of limitations required to gain title, as well as met the other elements of adverse possession required, such as they paid the 5 yrs taxes, they went to court to quiet title in Dec 1998. Homes Not Jails owned the home for almost 2 more years, until a judge overturned their claim to title in 2000…so now it sits empty again and the homeless are homeless again.

HOW TO SQUAT

A site out of Amsterdam called Krakengaatdoor (http://www.krakengaatdoor.nl/achtergrond-en.php) suggests the following squatting advice: "The squatting action itself begins with the breaking-open of the door and the placement inside of a table, bed and chair, the symbolic home furnishings which define domestic inviolability. Subsequently, the squatters call the police, who in turn come round to make a report. The police investigate the duration of vacancy, the owner, the plans for the space and other relevant matters . The officer of justice (prosecutor) subsequently determines whether the law has been broken (whether the premises have not been empty for a sufficiently long time) or whether the squatting is approved. If the premises were not empty for twelve months, then the squatters must vacate immediately. If the premises were in fact empty for long enough, then the authorities' concern is over with (for the time being) and the owner has to decide for himself how to deal with the situation. Most spaces that are 'legally' squatted have a 'life expectancy' of several months to perhaps even one or two years. A few percent stay squatted for longer, sometimes more than twenty years. Nowadays, premises are only evicted by the riot police a few times per year, all other squatting actions end peacefully."

The Squatters' Handbook (http://www.cat.org.au/housing/book.htm) out of Sydney, Australia, suggests checking "the overall structure of the place, are the gas and electricity meters still there? You need to know what to bring back to secure the house and fix it up if necessary…During the day on a weekday is actually the best time to check out houses, less conspicuous and you can see more. It can sometimes take quite some time for owners to realize that anyone is occupying the house, anything from a few hours to a day to a few weeks even. This time should be used for getting the house together, fixing things up, checking the wiring and water etc. It's a good idea to get services such as electricity and gas on as quickly as possible, so you can cook and maintain a life at your new home. First thing to do is change the locks and secure the house. Most barrel locks are easily replaced with a few tools (screwdriver, hacksaw, pliers etc.) and are available from hardware shops. Deadlocks may have to be sawn off and replaced totally, these cost more but are more secure. Doors or windows that can't be immediately repaired can have wood or board nailed on them to provide temporary security."

Homes Not Jails, in America, recommends, "The first thing to do is to make it look more of a home than a squat. Getting some furniture and possessions inside helps a lot. If the police come by and see that you're cooking dinner, reading or watching television they're much more likely to buy an argument that you have permission to be there and are really tenants. If it obviously looks like a squat you're just crashing in for the night, they're likely to ignore their training and procedures and will be happy to haul you off to the station "and let god and a judge sort it out later" (as one officer told squatters). The second thing to do is to get some utilities legally in your name and get some mail sent to your squat…This is relatively easy, since most utility companies don't assume you're squatting and won't ask for any proof of tenancy.

You should also have some mail sent to you and arrange for services like telephones and cable TV if you can afford them. Doing all this will give you a fistful of paper to show the police and raise serious doubts in their mind as to whether or not you're actually a trespasser. If you have a place looking like your home and have some mail and utility bills, you're likely to be successful in a face off with the police, even if the owner is there as well…In most cases, though, the first complaint will actually come from a neighbor who's suspicious…"

Another form of direct action with regards to land ownership is the Rent Strike. A zine out of Santa Cruz, CA entitled, "Pledge to Boycott Rent & Mortgage," advocates activists begin the organization of a city-wide rent strike. With 1,000 households pledging to boycott rent and mortgage, the first month would amass a budget of approximately $700,000 for legal fees to prevent eviction and to expand the rent strikes. Creative measures today, such as squatting and rent strikes, seem to be quite similar to moves made by other people in other times and places regarding housing and land ownership issues and Adverse Possession continues on in a few states to this day.

8 HOW TO INCLUDE THE POOR IN COMMUNITY EVENTS

Written by Kirsten Anderberg, 2004

It is not enough to say you would like more class diversity in whatever political group you affiliate with. The growth of the class chasm has gotten so precarious, that a reactive stance to classism is not enough. A proactive stance of class inclusion is required. Below are a few things that I think should always be done to try to include the widest range of economic classes, when it comes to organizing and participating in community events. "Community events" that constructively and effectively lock out the poor from participation are not really "community events," they are "exclusive" events. I think 5 things should always be in focus when organizing any event, if class diversity is truly desired: 1) The organizing meetings and events must take place on bus lines, 2) The organizing meetings must not take place at restaurants, 3) The organizing meetings and events must be kid-friendly or offer free childcare on premises, 4) There must be no membership fee to participate, 5) Charity may not be used as a way to skirt the first four rules.

Although the first rule, that all organizing meetings and events need to take place on bus lines, is obvious, many people are oblivious to this. So many middle class people drive, that they do not even think about buses. It is very important that the organizing meetings, not just the events themselves, take place on bus lines. If people cannot get to the organizing meetings due to no buses available, less people will participate in the event, as well. And rule 5 applies here as well. Do not try to offer rides to individual people because someone did not care enough to plan the meetings on bus lines. People will not participate if they cannot get there in an autonomous fashion. It just is a showing of dignity, that you recognize those taking buses are an important part of the congregation as well. Once my son was in a boy scout troop that was off the bus line. We had to walk forever in winter rain and sleet to get there at night! I hated it. Every now and then one of them would offer us a ride, but it was a constant hassle to arrange rides with these people I did not know them or share much of anything with their lifestyles, other than our kids were in the same classroom at school together. They were middle class, home owning, Christian Republicans, and I was not. So, it was uncomfortable for me to ride with them, I preferred walking in the rain. But it would have been cool if they had thought about people who walk and ride buses when choosing where to hold the meetings.

Rule two, do not have meetings and events at restaurants is essential, yet so often overlooked. I cannot tell you how many times I have not gone to meetings as soon as I found out they would be held at restaurants, as I did not have money for a restaurant. I would be counting my last $3 for the month and the idea of a restaurant was crazy. I also did not want to go through that weird awkward thing of telling them I could not go due to money, then them saying they would pitch in and buy my lunch. I would rather we just all met at a place where we all could have a pot luck lunch and all could easily participate without identifying our economic class. You never know who you are losing if you are doing organizing and events at restaurants, as the poor will not come, and they will not explain why either. Usually I just said my son was sick if I needed to get out of such a meeting. I remember a lot of that in law school. I was going to a club meeting, only to find out it was going to be at an expensive restaurant, and there went my participation. I remember not going to an LEIU protest wrap-up meeting last year because it was at a pizza place and I had no money.

Rule three, that the event must be kid-friendly or have childcare on premises, is also essential if you want a diverse class pool of women. Since I have rarely seen men hauling around children full time, but often see women doing so, I can tell you from personal experience that one of the things that isolated me as a mom was this childcare issue. Many single moms need more social interaction. They are living in poverty, they are working endlessly just to make survival, and there were many times I was interested in getting involved in things when I was a single mom, from musicals at my college, to political action, and I could not, due to childcare. Hell, when I was an early mom, you could not even work out or swim with a toddler. They finally caught on and put childcare in gyms and health clubs. There are even childcare areas at grocery stores and malls now, but in 1984, when I became a mom, no one had that together yet. Very few places were kid-friendly when I was a young mom. It has gotten better, but it is still a lonely world for single moms. Go to a library on a weekday in the children's section. You will see almost all women and children. Go to your local food bank. Now, that is where you will see almost all women and children exclusively. Those may be the women you will see show up if you include free childcare or make your events child friendly.

Rule four is do not collect membership fees. I mean that. I have not participated in many an organization due to membership fees. I did not participate in the Public Interest Law Foundation (PILF), which is Ralph Nader's baby, for public interest law work in law schools. It had a membership fee I could not afford. I asked Ralph directly if he could create something where low income people could join without the membership fee and he said he was not interested in that. He would come to my law school and PILF would sponsor $50 a plate dinners with Ralph. So even if I had raised the PILF membership fee, it seems I would not be able to participate in most of their events anyway! Another example is the PTA. At Northgate Elementary Public School, in Seattle, Wa., when my child attended, they charged membership fees to join the PTA, an organization which made all the decisions about what went on at the school, such as fund raisers, events, etc. So they told low income people that we could watch the PTA meetings, and come to the meetings, but we just could not vote on anything there! At a public school! I still find this to be outrageous! They then wanted to violate rule number 5, and try to hand pick who they would give PTA memberships to, etc., forcing the poor to identify themselves - it was a mess. Avoid all this. Just do not charge membership fees. Get outside funding, if you must. Do an extra fundraiser. But do not charge membership fees. And do not charge membership fees and then try to feign equality by saying if people identify themselves as low income you will give them a waiver. They should not have to identify themselves as poor to participate. Just avoid the fee altogether.

Rule five may not be deemed as important by the non-poor as it actually is. In 3 of the above 4 scenarios, people will try to violate those rules, in deference to charity. Charity is not dignity. Inclusion is dignity. Setting up an exclusive situation, then making people identify their income level if they cannot afford to participate at the exclusive level, but would still like to, is humiliating for the poor. Most poor folks would just not participate instead of making a fuss that they are poor and cannot afford a restaurant meeting or a membership fee. Most folks value autonomy, and if they cannot get there themselves, they will not go. If they cannot pay their way while there, they will not go. If you want to include the poor, meetings and events need mass transit accessibility, childcare or kid-friendly environments, no membership fees, and meeting places where paying for food is not involved. And those conditions need to be met without exception, without charity as a means to try to avoid them. The charity is demeaning. Just include the poor in the planning instead.

For more articles written by Kirsten Anderberg, visit www.kirstenanderberg.com. You can contact Kirsten Anderberg at kirstenaATresist,ca.

Printed in Great Britain
by Amazon